**2018**

MASTERPIECE QUILTING'S

# Christmas
## COLLECTION

### NANCY SCOTT

*Masterpiece Quilting's 2018 Christmas Collection*
Copyright © 2018 by Masterpiece Quilting, LLC .

Book Design: Page + Pixel
Photography: Danielle Morales of InJoy Photography
Photo Stylists: Abigail Hake Kellermeyer & Tammi Hake

All rights reserved.

No part of this book may be reproduced in any form or by any electronic or mechanical means including information storage and retrieval systems without permission in writing from the publisher, except by a reviewer who may quote brief passages in a review.

ISBN 978-0-692-19916-9

Manufactured in the United States.

11   12   13   14   15     5   4   3   2   1

## Table of Contents

Introduction...5

### Dining Room Décor
Let's Gather Table Runner...7
Wreath Runner & Wall Hanging...11
Holly Table Topper...19
Mugs Rugs & Coaster...23

### Beautiful Bedrooms
Poinsettia Bed Runner & Pillow...27
Jingle Bells Quilt...31
Jingle Bells Wall Hanging...37

### Lovely Living Rooms
Mistletoe Magic Throw & Pillow...41
Tree of Presents Wall Hanging...47
O Christmas Tree Wall Hanging...53
Friendship Stars Throw...57

About the Author...64

## Introduction

Decorating for the Holidays fits into one of two categories. For some people, it is a glorious event – which they live for, plan all year for and thoroughly enjoy. And for the rest of us, our goal is to get it done as quickly and as painlessly as possible sometimes within minutes of guests arriving!

As I designed each of the projects for this book, I focused on getting the most impact out of each piece as possible. Regardless of your decorating style, there is something in this book that is sure to please. I've divided the projects based on the primary areas of the home – dining room, bedroom and living room. The holidays are traditionally associated with celebratory meals and the projects in this book will have your dining room set for any occasion. Regardless of whether you have guests spending the night or the bed is simply a gathering place for coats and hats, your bedroom will be seasonally styling with these options. And for those who sit and visit, your living room will be comfortable and inviting.

**Project Notes:**

- Read all instructions before beginning each project.
- Fabric quantities and cutting instructions are based on 40″ useable width of fabric for yardage and 20″ for fat quarters.
- All seams are sewn right sides of fabric together with ¼″ seam allowances unless noted.

DINING ROOM

# LET'S GATHER TABLE RUNNER

When family and friends gather, nothing sets the mood better than a beautiful table runner. The length of this runner can easily be adjusted by changing the number of blocks in the center section.

# Let's Gather Table Runner

**CONFIDENT BEGINNER**

**FINISHED RUNNER SIZE:** 16½" × 72"  **FINISHED BLOCK SIZE:** 12" × 12"  **NUMBER OF BLOCKS:** 5

## SUPPLIES

- ¼ yard gold tonal
- ⅓ yard red tonal
- ¾ yard beige tonal
- 1⅛ yards green tonal
- 2¼ yards of 40" wide fabric for backing
- Batting to Size*
- Basic quilting tools and sewing supplies

*Warm 80/20 Batting from The Warm Company used to make sample.*

## CUTTING INSTRUCTIONS

### From gold tonal:
- Cut 1 (3⅞" by WOF) strip.

  Subcut strip into 10 (3⅞") squares. Cut each square in half on one diagonal to make 20 E triangles.

### From red tonal:
- Cut 2 (3⅞" by WOF) strip.

  Subcut strip into 20 (3⅞") squares. Cut each square in half on one diagonal to make 40 F triangles.

### From beige tonal:
- Cut 1 (3⅞" by WOF) strip.

  Subcut strip into 10 (3⅞") C squares.

- Cut 2 (7¼" by WOF) strips.

  Subcut strips into 6 (7¼") squares. Cut each square on both diagonals to make 24 triangles; discard 2 leaving 22 D triangles.

### From green tonal:
- Cut 1 (4¾" by WOF) strip

  Subcut strip into 5 (4¾") A squares.

- Cut 1 (3⅞" by WOF) strip.

  Subcut strip into 10 (3⅞") B squares.

- Cut 1 (2½" by WOF) strip.

  Subcut strip into 2 (2½" × 7½") G and 2 (2½" × 10") H strips.

- Cut 3 (2⅝" × WOF) I strips.

- Cut 5 (2½" × WOF) binding strips.

**DINING ROOM**
Let's Gather Table Runner

# Block Construction

**1.** Arrange and sew E triangles to opposite sides of an A square; press. Sew E triangles to the remaining two sides to complete an A-E unit; press. Trim unit, if needed, to measure 6½″ square. Repeat to make 5 A-E units.

**2.** Draw a diagonal line from corner to corner on the wrong side of each C square.

**3.** With right sides together, pair a C and B square together and stitch ¼″ on each side of the drawn line. Cut on the drawn line to make 2 B-C units; press. Trim unit, if needed, to measure 3½″ square. Repeat to make 20 B-C units.

**4.** Arrange and stitch an F triangle to one short side of a D triangle; press. Stitch a second F triangle to the opposite side to make a D-F unit; press. Trim unit, if needed, to measure 3½″ × 6½″. Repeat to make 20 D-F units.

**5.** Arrange 4 B-C, 4 D-F and 1 A-E unit into three rows of three units each. Sew units into rows, then sew rows together to complete one block; press. Repeat to make 5 blocks.

*Masterpiece Quilting's 2018 Christmas Collection*

## END TRIANGLE

**1.** Sew a G strip to one short side of a D triangle; press.

**2.** Sew an H strip to the opposite short side of D; press. Trim ends of G and H strips even with the long edge of D to make an end triangle; press. **FIG A**

**3.** Repeat steps 1 and 2 to make a second end triangle.

## Quilt Top Assembly

**1.** Following the Assembly Diagram, arrange and stitch the blocks and end triangles into a row; press.

**2.** Sew the I strips together on the short ends to make one long strip. Subcut strip into 2 (2⅝" × 62") I strips.

**3.** Center and sew I strips to opposite long sides of the pieced center. Trim ends of I strips even with the angles edges of end triangles to complete the table runner top; press.

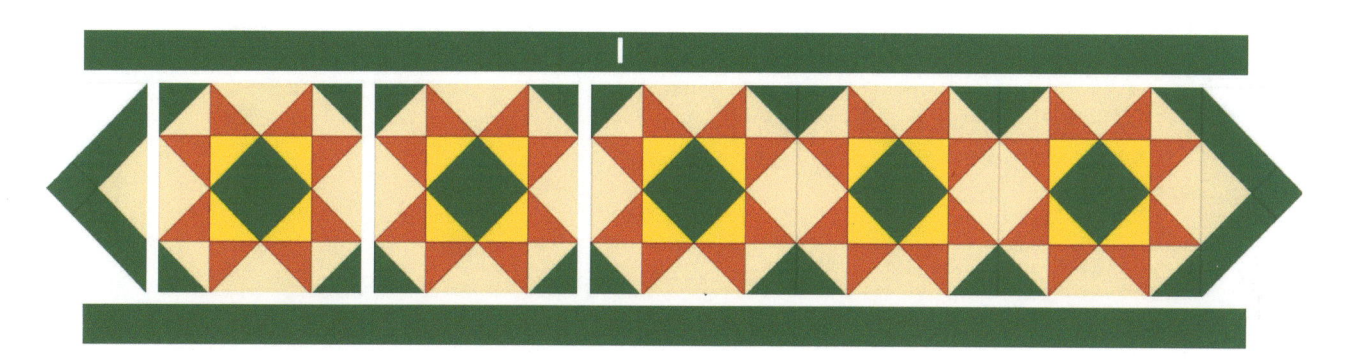

A.

## Finishing the Quilt

**1.** Layer the quilt top, batting and backing and quilt as desired. Sample quilt was custom quilted with curved arcs to accentuate the piecing.

**2.** Stitch binding strips together end to end using diagonal seams. Fold and press the resulting long strip in half lengthwise with wrong sides together. Stitch to quilt, matching raw edges and mitering corners.

**3.** Fold the binding to the reverse side and hand or machine stitch in place.

DINING ROOM
Let's Gather Table Runner

# WREATH RUNNER & WALL HANGING

This duo will make your Holiday decorating super simple. Whether gracing the center of the table or a buffet this runner spreads Holiday cheer in style. The wall hanging completes the ensemble to make your décor the envy of the neighborhood.

# Wreath Runner & Wall Hanging

CONFIDENT BEGINNER

### RUNNER
FINISHED SIZE: 15″ × 53″   FINISHED BLOCK SIZE: 8″ × 8″   NUMBER OF BLOCKS: 5

### WALL HANGING
FINISHED SIZE: 25″ × 25″   FINISHED BLOCK SIZE: 16″ × 16″   NUMBER OF BLOCKS: 1

## SUPPLIES

*Makes 1 Runner and Wall Hanging*

- 12–14 precut 10″ squares of assorted green tonals, prints and solids
- 1 fat quarter red dot
- 1 yard white tonal
- 1¼ yard red print
- 2½ yards of 40″ wide fabric for backing
- Batting to Size*
- Fusible web with paper release*
- Template material
- Basic quilting tools and sewing supplies

*\* Warm 80/20 Batting and Lite Steam-A-Seam 2 Fusible Web from The Warm Company were used to make the sample quilt.*

## CUTTING INSTRUCTIONS

### From green precut squares:
- Cut 76 (2½″) A squares.
- Cut 4 (2⅞″) squares; subcut each square in half on one diagonal to make 8 B triangles.
- Cut 4 (3⅞″) C squares.
- Cut 20 (2″) D squares.
- Cut 20 (2⅞″) E squares.

### From white tonal:
- Cut 2 (2½″ by WOF) strips.

  Subcut strips into 2 each 2½″ × 16½″ J strips and 2½″ × 20½″ K strips.

- Cut 1 (8½″ by WOF) strip.

  Subcut strip into 1 (8½″) F square and 6 (2″ × 8½″) L strips.

- Cut 1 (2⅞″ × WOF) strip.

  Subcut strip into 10 (2⅞″) H squares

- Cut 2 (2″ by WOF) M strips.
- Cut 1 (4⅞″ by WOF) strip.

  Subcut strip into 2 (4⅞″) squares. Cut each square in half on one diagonal to make 4 I triangles.

  Trim remainder of strip to 4½″ width and subcut 5 (4½″) G squares.

### From red print:
- Cut 4 (3″ by WOF) strips.

  Subcut strips into 4 (3″ × 28″) P strips.

- Cut 4 (2½″ by WOF) binding strips for runner.
- Cut 3 (2½″ by WOF) binding strips for wall hanging.

DINING ROOM
Wreath Runner & Wall Hanging

|  | A squares | B triangles | C squares | D squares | E squares | F squares | G squares | H squares | I triangles | J strips | K strips | L strips | M strips | N/O strips | P strips |
|---|---|---|---|---|---|---|---|---|---|---|---|---|---|---|---|
| Table Runner | 4- | - | - | 20 | 20 | - | 5 | 10 | - | - | - | 6 | 3 | 4 | - |
| Wall Hanging | 36 | 8 | 4 | - | - | 1 | - | - | 4 | 2 | 2 | - | - | - | 4 |

## Runner Block Construction

**1.** Draw a diagonal line from corner to corner on the wrong side of each D and H square.

**2.** Pair an E and H square together and stitch ¼" away the drawn line on both sides. Cut on the drawn line and press open to make two E-H units. Trim units, if needed, to measure 2½" square. Repeat to make a total of 20 E-H units.

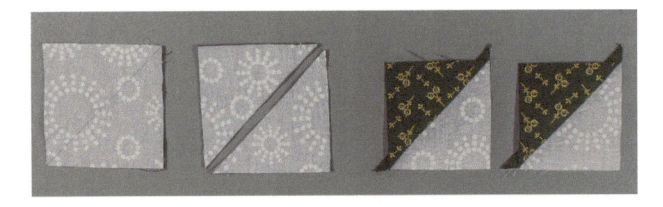

**3.** Sew two A squares together to make an A-A unit as shown; press. Repeat to make a total of 20 A-A units.

**4.** Position a D square on one corner of a G square, stitch of the drawn line and trim ¼" away from stitching line as shown. Flip D away from G and press.

**5.** Repeat step 4, stitching, trimming and pressing D squares on each corner of each G square to make a total of 5 D-G units. Trim, if needed, each unit to measure 4½" square.

12 Masterpiece Quilting's *2018 Christmas Collection*

**6.** Arrange and sew an A-A unit to opposite sides of a D-G unit to make a block center section; press. Repeat to make a total of 5 block center sections.

**7.** Sew an E-H unit to opposite ends of an A-A unit to make a top / bottom row as shown; press. Repeat to make a total of 10 rows.

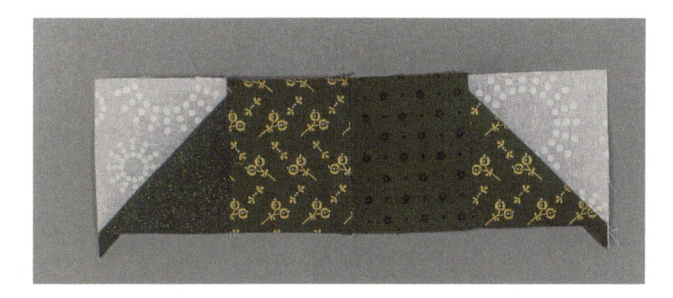

**8.** Sew rows to the top and bottom of a block center section to complete a runner block as shown; press. Repeat to make a total of 5 runner blocks.

## RUNNER TOP ASSEMBLY

**1.** Alternately sew six L strips and five runner blocks into a horizontal row; press.

**2.** Sew M strips together on short ends to make one long strip; press. Subcut strip into 2 (2″ × 44″) M strips.

**3.** Sew M strips to top and bottom of pieced center section; press.

**4.** Join N / O strips together on short ends to make one long strip. Subcut strip into 2 each 2½″ × 56″ O strips and 2½″ × 18″ N strips.

**5.** Center and sew N strips to opposite short ends and O strips to both long sides of runner starting and stopping ¼″ from each end of the pieced center. Miter corners, trim and press.

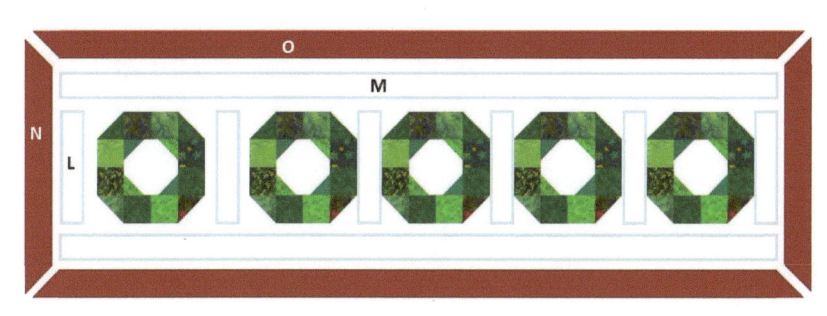

**DINING ROOM**
**Wreath Runner & Wall Hanging**

# Wall Hanging Block Construction

**1.** Draw a diagonal line from corner to corner on the wrong side of each C square.

**2.** Position a C square on one corner of F, stitch on the drawn line and trim ¼″ away from stitch line as shown. Flip C away from F and press.

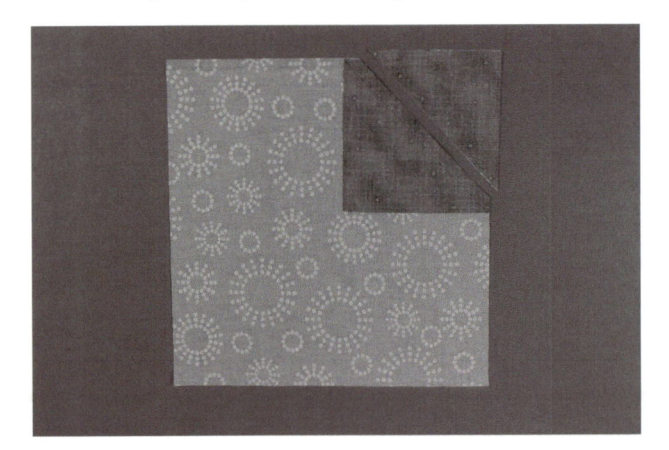

**3.** Repeat step 2, stitching, trimming and pressing a C square on each corner of F to make a C-F unit. Trim unit, if needed, to measure 8½″ × 8½″ square.

**4.** Arrange and stitch 8 A squares into two rows of four squares each. Stitch rows together to form an 8-patch unit as shown; press. Repeat to make a total of four 8-patch units.

**5.** Sew an 8-patch unit onto opposite sides of a C-F unit to make the block center section; press.

**6.** Arrange and stitch B triangles onto adjacent sides of an A square as shown to make an A-B unit; press. Repeat to make a total of four A-B units.

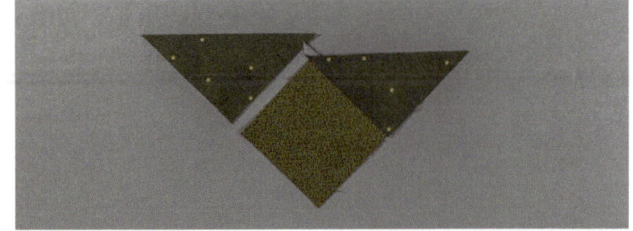

**7.** Arrange and stitch an I triangle to an A-B unit to make an A-B-I square as shown; press. Trim unit, if needed, to measure 4½″ square. Repeat to make a total of four A-B-I squares.

14  Masterpiece Quilting's 2018 Christmas Collection

**8.** Sew an A-B-I square to opposite ends of an 8-patch unit to make a top / bottom row; press. Repeat to make a second top / bottom row.

**9.** Arrange and stitch rows to top and bottom of block center section to complete the wreath block; press.

## WALL HANGING ASSEMBLY

**1.** Sew J strips to opposite sides and K strips to top and bottom of wreath block; press.

**2.** Center and sew P strips to all four sides of pieced center starting and stopping ¼" from each end. Miter corners, trim and press to complete the wreath top.

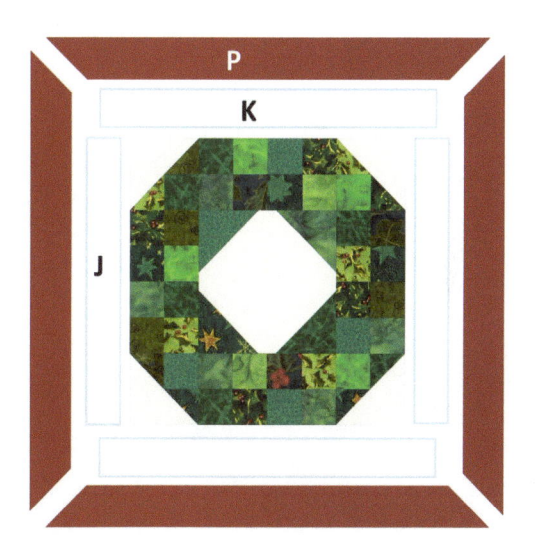

# Adding the Appliques

**1.** Prepare provided applique motif pieces using your preferred method. Note: the included applique templates are sized to scale.

**2.** Trace the indicated number of each shape onto the paper side of the fusible web, reversing the template were indicated.

**3.** Cut out each piece leaving a ¼" margin around each.

**4.** Following the manufacturer's directions, fuse appliques pieced to the wrong side of the red pin dot fabric. When complete you should have the following:

- 1 Wall Hanging bow, 1 Wall Hanging bow reversed
- 1 Wall Hanging knot
- 1 Wall Hanging streamer, 1 Wall Hanging streamer reversed
- 5 Runner bows, 5 Runner bows reversed
- 5 Runner knots
- 5 Runner streamers, 5 Runner streamers reversed

**DINING ROOM**
**Wreath Runner & Wall Hanging**

**5.** Cut each fabric-interfacing piece along the drawn line and remove paper backing.

**6.** On an ironing surface, press the pieced wreath top, then arrange applique pieces on the lower section of the wreath referring to the project photo. Tuck the bow and streamer ends under the bow center.

**7.** Fuse in place following manufacturer's instructions.

**8.** Repeat steps 6-7 on the pieced runner top.
**Note:** The position of the bows can be changed if you prefer to use the runner as a vertical wall hanging.

**9.** Stitch around each piece to secure raw edges. The sample quilts were stitching using contrasting thread and a machine applique (blanket) stitch.

**10.** Press both sides of the runner and wreath top.

## Finishing the Quilts

**1.** Layer the quilt top, batting and backing and quilt as desired. The sample quilts were custom quilted with free motion meander in the center section and straight lines in the borders.

**2.** Stitch binding strips together end to end using diagonal seams. Fold and press the resulting long strip in half lengthwise with wrong sides together. Stitch to quilt, matching raw edges and mitering corners.

**3.** Fold the binding to the reverse side and hand- or machine-stitch in place.

DINING ROOM
Wreath Runner & Wall Hanging

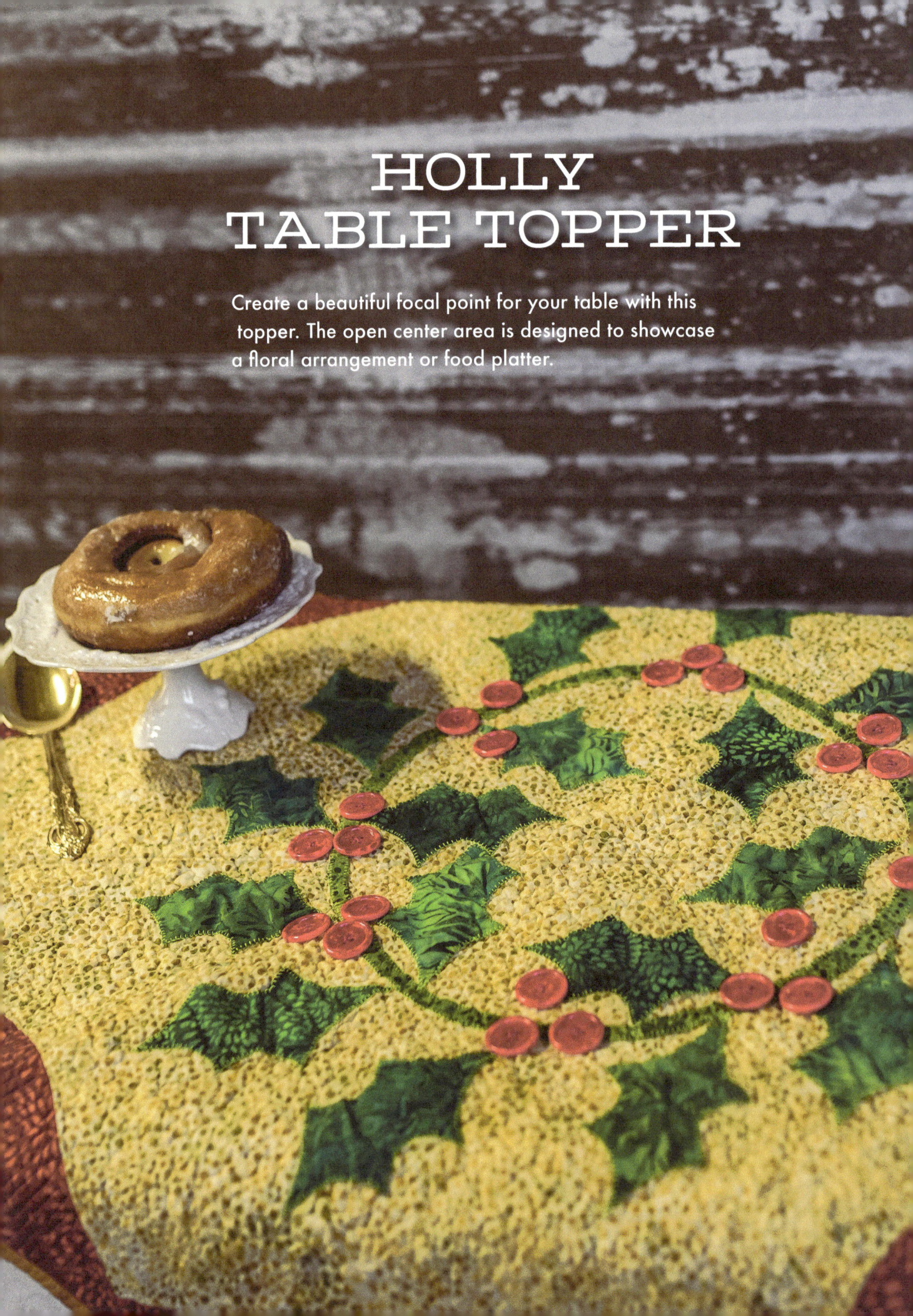

# HOLLY TABLE TOPPER

Create a beautiful focal point for your table with this topper. The open center area is designed to showcase a floral arrangement or food platter.

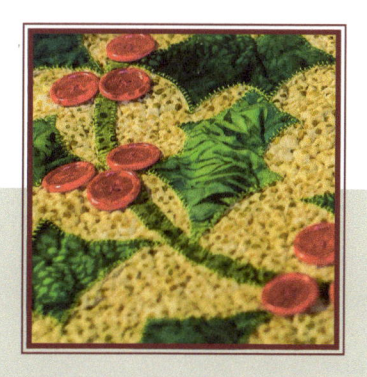

# Holly Table Topper

### INTERMEDIATE

**FINISHED RUNNER SIZE:** 33″ × 33″

## SUPPLIES

- 1 fat quarter green batik for leaves*
- 1 fat quarter green batik for vine*
- ⅝ yard gold batik*
- ¾ yards red batik*
- 1 yard beige batik*
- 1⅛ yards of 40″ wide fabric for backing
- Batting to Size*
- Fusible web with paper release*
- Template material
- 24 ¾″ red buttons for holly berries**
- Basic quilting tools and sewing supplies

*Batik fabrics from Island Batik, Warm 80/20 Batting and Lite Steam-A-Seam 2 Fusible Web from The Warm Company were used to make the sample quilt.*

**Note: Buttons can be choking hazards for both small children and pets. If the table topper will be used around either, they should be omitted and red circles can be appliqued or embroidered instead.**

## CUTTING INSTRUCTIONS

Prepare provided cutting template using your preferred method. **Note:** the cutting template is sized to scale.

### From green batik for vine:
- Cut 1½″ bias strips to total 48″ when seamed together.

### From gold batik:
- Cut 4 (2½″ × WOF) binding strips.

### From red batik:
- Cut 4 (2″ × WOF) strips. Subcut strips into 2 (2″ × 30″) C and 2 (2″ × 33½″) D strips.
- Cut 12 B pieces using provided template.

### From beige batik:
- Cut 1 (30″ × WOF) strip. Subcut strip into 1 (30″ × 30″) A square.

**DINING ROOM**
Holly Table Topper

## Quilt Top Assembly

**1.** Light starch and press the A square. Using the cutting template, align the straight edge of the template with the raw edge of the square. Draw and cut three arcs on each side of the square leaving a ½" spacing between each arc and the corners.

**2.** Arrange and stitch a B piece in each cutout arc on the A square to make an A-B unit; press.

**3.** Sew C strips to opposite sides and D strips to the top and bottom of the A-B unit to complete the quilt top; press.

## Adding the Appliques

**1.** To prepare the vines, sew the long edges of the seamed bias strip together with wrong sides facing and a ¼" seam allowance. Trim seam allowance to ⅛" and press the seam open, centering the seam along the back of the vine.

**2.** Mark a 13" diameter circle in the middle of the quilt top. Pin the vine to cover the marked circle, tucking under raw edges on both ends.

**3.** Stitch around both sides of the vine to secure. The sample quilt was stitched using matching thread and a machine applique (blanket) stitch.

**4.** Prepare provided applique holly leaf pattern using your preferred method. Note: the included applique shape is sized to scale.

**5.** Trace 18 holly leaves onto the paper side of the fusible web.

**6.** Cut out each piece leaving a ¼" margin around each.

**7.** Following the manufacturer's directions, fuse appliques to the wrong side of the green batik fabric.

**8.** Cut each fabric-interfacing piece along the drawn line and remove paper backing.

**9.** On an ironing surface, press the top, then arrange applique pieces referring to the project photo.

**10.** Fuse in place following manufacturer's instructions.

20  *Masterpiece Quilting's 2018 Christmas Collection*

**11.** Stitch around each piece to secure raw edges. The sample quilt was stitched using matching thread and a machine applique (blanket) stitch.

**12.** Press both sides of the topper

## Finishing the Quilt

**1.** Layer the quilt top, batting and backing and quilt as desired. The sample quilt was custom quilted with a free motion meander around the appliques and straight line stitching in the borders and arcs.

**2.** Stitch binding strips together end to end using diagonal seams. Fold and press the resulting long strip in half lengthwise with wrong sides together. Stitch to trimmed quilt, matching raw edges and mitering corners.

**3.** Fold the binding to the reverse side and hand- or machine-stitch in place.

**4.** Arrange and sew buttons in clusters of three to represent holly berries.

# MUG RUGS & COASTERS

It can't be a gathering without food and beverage. Mug Rugs are perfect for guests to set their snack on while visiting and coasters are the perfect landing spot for a drink. This is a great way to use up scraps from any of the projects and have accessories that match a throw or a topper.

# Mug Rugs & Coasters

BEGINNER

FINISHED MUG RUG SIZE: 6½" × 6½"   FINISHED COASTER SIZE: 5" diameter

## SUPPLIES

### Mug Rugs
- 9 – 2½" A squares in assorted seasonal colors: red, green and gold
- 1 – 6½" backing square
- 1 – 2½" × 40" gold tonal binding strip
- 1 – 6½" square of double sided fusible foam
- Basic quilting tools and sewing supplies

### Coaster
- Scraps of assorted seasonal prints
- 1 – 6" backing square
- 2½" × 20" red tonal bias binding strip
- Scrap of batting*
- Template Material
- Basic quilting tools and sewing supplies

*Warm 80/20 batting from The Warm Company used to make sample coaster.*

DINING ROOM
Mug Rugs & Coasters   23

## Assembling the Mug Rug

**1.** Arrange the A squares into 3 rows of 3 squares each.

**2.** Sew squares together into rows and sew rows together to complete the mug rug top; press.

**3.** Layer the backing square with wrong side up, fusible foam and the mug rug top with right side up. Align raw edges.

**4.** Fuse all three layers together referring to manufacturer's instructions.

### FINISHING THE MUG RUG

**1.** Quilt mug rug as desired or not at all.

**2.** Stitch binding strips together end to end using diagonal seams. Fold and press the resulting long strip in half lengthwise with wrong sides together. Stitch to trimmed quilt, matching raw edges and mitering corners.

**3.** Fold the binding to the reverse side and hand- or machine-stitch in place.

## Assembling the Coaster

**1.** Improvisationally piece scraps to make at least a 6″ square.

**2.** Prepare provided circle cutting pattern using your preferred method. Note: the included pattern is sized to scale.

**3.** Center and mark the circle on pieced square. Cut out using scissors or alternately, use a 5″ die cutting machine.

**4.** Repeat step 3 to cut batting and backing to the same size as coaster top.

### FINISHING THE COASTER

**1.** Layer the coaster top, batting and backing and quilt as desired. The sample coaster was straight line stitched ¼″ from piecing seams.

**2.** Stitch binding strips together end to end using diagonal seams. Fold and press the resulting long strip in half lengthwise with wrong sides together. Stitch to trimmed quilt, matching raw edges.

**3.** Fold the binding to the reverse side and hand- or machine-stitch in place.

DINING ROOM
Mug Rugs & Coasters

25

## BED ROOMS

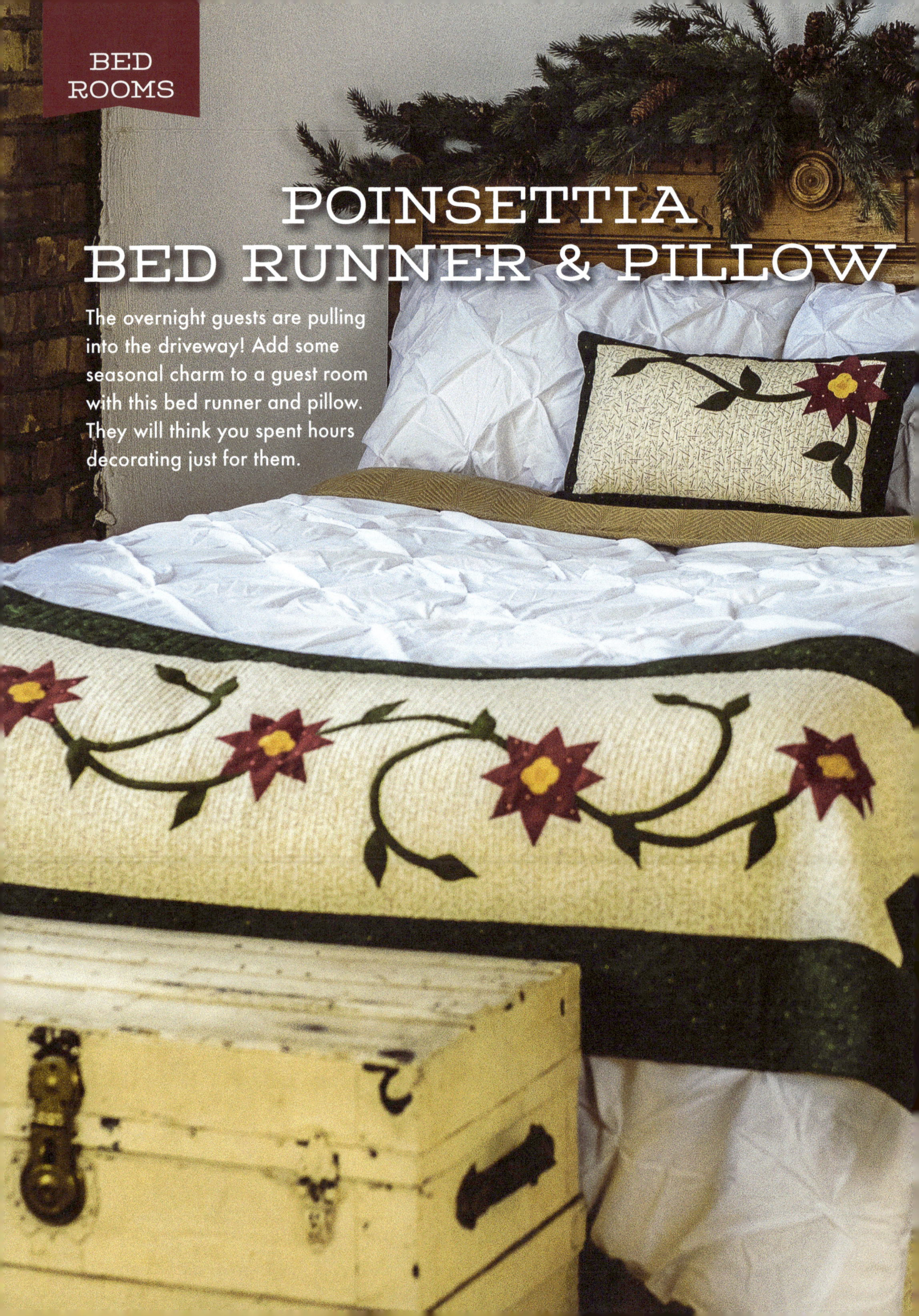

# POINSETTIA BED RUNNER & PILLOW

The overnight guests are pulling into the driveway! Add some seasonal charm to a guest room with this bed runner and pillow. They will think you spent hours decorating just for them.

## Poinsettia Bed Runner & Pillow

**CONFIDENT BEGINNER**

FINISHED RUNNER SIZE: 25″ × 73″   FINISHED PILLOW SIZE: 12″ × 20″

### SUPPLIES

*Makes 1 Runner and Pillow*

- Small pieces of gold and red prints, solids and tonals
- ½ yard green tonal for vines and leaves
- 1¾ yards green dot
- 1⅞ yards beige print
- 2¼ yards of 40″ wide fabric for runner backing
- Batting to Size*
- Fusible web with paper release*
- Template material
- 12″ × 20″ Pillow Form
- Basic quilting tools and sewing supplies

*Warm 80/20 Batting and Lite Steam-A-Seam 2 Fusible Web from The Warm Company were used to make the sample quilt.

### CUTTING INSTRUCTIONS

**From green tonal:**
- Cut 1½″ bias strips to total 120″ when seamed together.

**From green dot:**
- Cut 2 (2½″ by WOF) strips.

  Subcut strips into 2 each 2½″ × 9½″ B strips and 2½″ × 21½″ C strips.

- Cut 5 (5½″ by WOF) strips.

  Subcut strips into 2 each 5½″ × 15½″ E strips and 5½″ × 73½″ F strips.

- Cut 1 (13¼″ by WOF) strip.

  Subcut strip into 2 (13¼″ × 15″) pillow backing rectangles.

- Cut 5 (2½″ by WOF) binding strips.

**From beige print:**
- Cut 1 (63½″ by WOF) strip.

  Subcut 1 (15½″ × 63½″) D and 1 (9½″ × 17½″) A rectangle.

BEDROOM
Poinsettia Bed Runner & Pillow   27

## Assembling the Bed Runner

Sew E strips to opposite sides and F strips to the top and bottom of the D rectangle; press.

## Assembling the Pillow

Sew B strips to opposite sides and C strips to the top and bottom of the A rectangle; press.

## Adding the Appliques

**1.** To prepare the vines, sew the long edges of the seamed bias strip together with wrong sides facing and a ¼″ seam allowance. Trim seam allowance to ⅛″ and press the seam open, centering the seam along the back of the vine.

**2.** Mark placement lines for the vines and poinsettia clusters on the pillow and runner top referring to the project photos and placement diagrams.

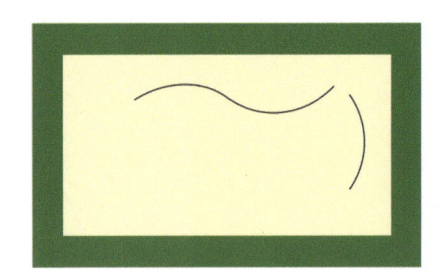

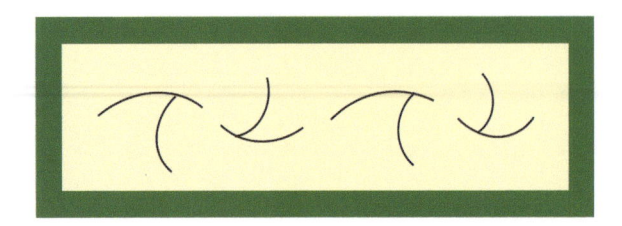

**3.** Prepare provided applique patterns using your preferred method. Note: the included applique shapes are sized to scale.

**4.** Trace the number indicated of each shape onto the paper side of the fusible web.

**5.** Cut out each piece leaving a ¼″ margin around each.

**6.** Following the manufacturer's directions, fuse appliques to the wrong side of fabrics as listed below.

**RED TONAL:** 24 poinsettia petals

**RED DOT:** 24 poinsettia petals

**GOLD #1:** 6 poinsettia centers

**GOLD #2:** 6 poinsettia buds

**GREEN TONAL:** 22 leaves

**7.** Cut each fabric-interfacing piece along the drawn line and remove paper backing.

**8.** On an ironing surface, press the top, then cut and pin the vine over the drawn placement lines. Note: the vine doesn't have to completely extend under the poinsettia cluster, it can just be tucked under each side. The leaves and poinsettia petals will cover the raw ends of the vine. Layout the leaves, poinsettia petals, centers and buds to confirm placement.

**9.** When satisfied with the placement, remove leaves and poinsettia pieces and stitch both sides of the vine to secure. The sample projects were stitched using matching thread and a machine applique (blanket) stitch.

**10.** Reposition leaves, poinsettia petals, centers and buds. Fuse in place following manufacturer's instructions.

**11.** Stitch around each piece to secure raw edges. The sample projects were stitched using matching thread and a machine applique (blanket) stitch.

**12.** Press both sides of the pillow and runner top.

## Finishing the Bed Runner

**1.** Layer the runner top, batting and backing and quilt as desired. The sample runner was custom quilted with straight line stitched around the applique and a customer border.

**2.** Stitch binding strips together end to end using diagonal seams. Fold and press the resulting long strip in half lengthwise with wrong sides together. Stitch to trimmed quilt, matching raw edges and mitering corners.

**3.** Fold the binding to the reverse side and hand- or machine-stitch in place.

## Finishing the Pillow

You can either quilt the pillow top before adding the back or leave it un-quilted. If you prefer to leave it un-quilted, skip Step 1.

**1.** If desired; layer pillow top, right side up over batting and lining. Baste or pin. Quilt as desired. Sample was quilted with vertical straight lines around the appliques. Trim batting and lining ¼″ beyond raw edge of pillow top.

**2.** To make an envelope back for the pillow, press and stitch a ½″ double hem on one short side of each backing rectangle.

**3.** Place pillow front right side up and position one square at the top, right side down, matching top raw edges with a hemmed side toward the center. Place the second square at the bottom edge, right side down, matching raw edges at the bottom and overlapping the first square.

**4.** Stitch all around with a ⅜″ seam allowance. Turn right side out through the overlapped opening.

**5.** Insert the pillow form into the pillowcase to finish.

**BEDROOM**
Poinsettia Bed Runner & Pillow

# JINGLE BELLS QUILT

This quilt will be the focal point of any bedroom as you celebrate Christmas in style.

## Jingle Bells Quilt

CONFIDENT BEGINNER

FINISHED QUILT SIZE: 80″ × 80″    FINISHED BLOCK SIZE: 10″ × 10″    NUMBER OF BLOCKS: 25

### SUPPLIES

- ½ yard dark gold tonal
- 1½ yards medium gold tonal
- 2 yards red dot including binding
- 2 yards green print
- 4¾ yards off-white solid
- 2½ yards of 40″ wide fabric for backing
- Batting to Size*
- Fusible web with Paper release*
- Template Material
- Thread to match appliques
- 9 yards ¼″ gold trim
- ½″ yellow buttons or gold bells**
- Basic quilting tools and sewing supplies

* Warm 80/20 Batting and Lite Steam-A-Seam 2 Fusible Web from The Warm Company were used to make the sample quilt.

** **Note:** Buttons and bells can be choking hazards for both small children and pets. If the quilt will be used around either, they should be omitted.

### CUTTING INSTRUCTIONS

**From medium gold tonal:**
- Cut 3 (4⅞″ by WOF) strips; subcut strips into 24 (4⅞″) B squares.

**From red dot:**
- Cut 2 (2½″ by WOF) strips; subcut strips into 25 (2½″) D squares.
- Cut 9 (2½″ by WOF) binding strips.

**From green print:**
- Cut 7 (4⅞″ by WOF) strips; subcut strips into 50 (4⅞″) A squares.

**From white solid:**
- Cut 7 (4½″ by WOF) strips; subcut strips into 100 (2½″ × 4½″) C strips.
- Cut 4 (4⅞″ by WOF) strips; subcut strips into 26 (4⅞″) B squares.
- Cut 1 (60½″ × WOF) strip; subcut strip into 4 (10½″ × 60½″) G strips
- Cut 1 (10½″ × WOF) strip; subcut strip into 4 (10½″) H squares
- Cut 6 (5½″ × WOF) E / F strips

BEDROOM
Jingle Bells Quilt    31

## Block Construction

**1.** Draw a diagonal line from corner to corner on the wrong side of each B square.

**2.** Pair an A and B square with right sides together and stitch ¼" on both sides of the drawn line. Cut on the drawn line and press open to make two green-gold A-B units. Repeat to make a total of 48 green-gold A-B units.

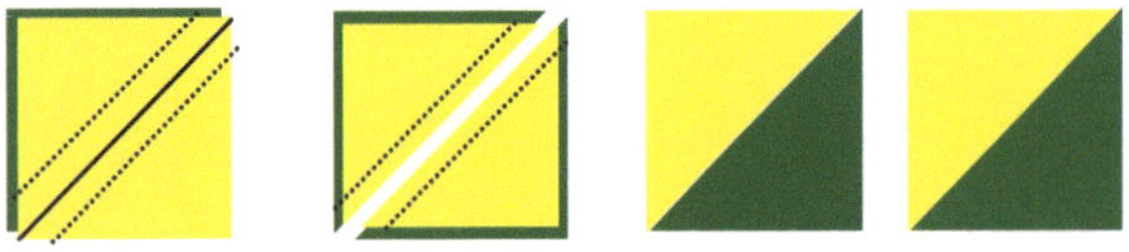

**3.** Repeat Step 2 to make a total of 26 green-white A-B units.

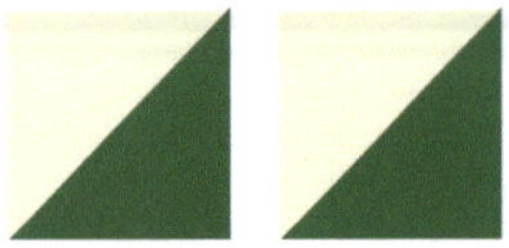

**4.** Arrange and stitch a D square between two C strips to make a C-D unit; press. Repeat to make a total of 25 C-D strips.

**5.** To make Block 1, select three green-white A-B units, one green-gold A-B unit, one C-D unit and two C strips. Arrange the units and strips into three rows as shown.

**6.** Stitch units and strips into rows and stitch rows together to complete a Block 1; press. Repeat to make a total of four Block 1's.

**7.** To make Block 2, select two each green-white and green-gold A-B units, one C-D unit and two C strips. Arrange the units and strips into three rows as shown.

**8.** Stitch units and strips into rows and stitch rows together to complete a Block 2; press. Repeat to make a total of 16 Block 2's.

**9.** To make Block 3, select one green-white, three green-gold A-B units, one C-D unit and two C strips. Arrange the units and strips into three rows as shown.

**10.** Stitch units and strips into rows and stitch rows together to complete a Block 3; press. Repeat to make a total of four Block 3's.

**11.** To make Block 4, select four green-white A-B units, one C-D unit and two C strips. Arrange the units and strips into three rows as shown.

**12.** Stitch units and strips into rows and stitch rows together to complete a Block 4; press.

**BEDROOM**
**Jingle Bells Quilt**

## Assembling the Quilt Center

**1.** Referring to the Assembly Diagram, arrange Blocks 1, 2, 3, and 4 into five rows of five blocks each. Stitch the blocks into rows and stitch the rows together to complete the pieced center; press. The pieced center should measure 50½″ × 50½″

**2.** Sew E/F strips together in the short ends to make one long strip; press. Subcut strip into two each 5½″ × 50½″ E and 5½″ × 60½″ F strips.

**3.** Sew the E strips to opposite sides and F strips to the top and bottom of the pieced center to complete the quilt top center. The quilt top center should measure 60½″ × 60½″.

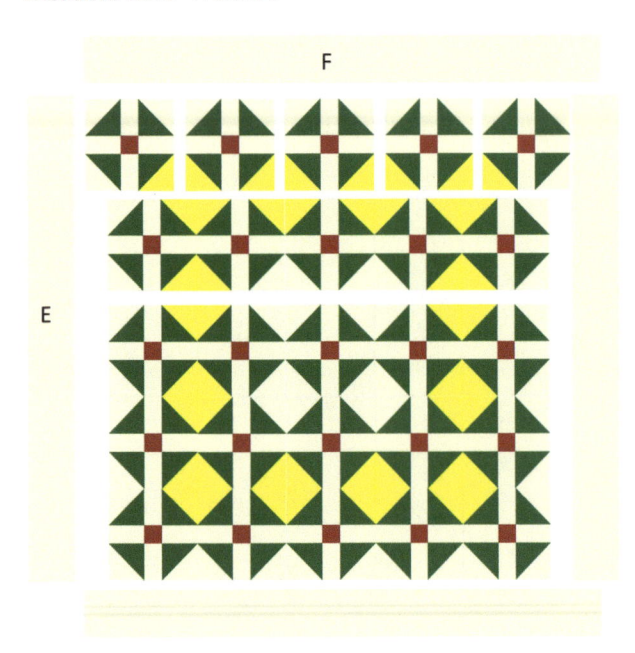

## Completing the Appliqued Borders and Corners

**1.** Prepare templates for each applique motif provided. Note: the included applique templates are sized to scale.

**2.** Trace each shape onto the paper side of the fusible web referring to the number needed as listed in Step 4.

**3.** Cut out each shape leaving a ¼″ margin around each.

**4.** Fuse each shape onto the wrong side of the fabric as listed.

**Green Print:** 20 full swags, 8 half swags and 4 corner swags

**Red Print:** 48 bows, 24 reversed; 48 streamers, 24 reversed; 24 knots

**Medium Gold:** 24 large bells, 48 small bells

**Dark Gold:** 24 large inner bells, 48 small inner bells

**5.** Cut out each shape on the drawn line and remove paper backing.

**6.** On an ironing surface, press a G strip flat. Measure 2½″ down from the top long side of G and draw an orientation line. Referring to the photo for positioning, arrange five full and two half swags on G with the tips positioned along the orientation line. Fuse in place following manufacturer's instructions. Machine blanket stitch with matching thread.

**7.** Arrange bells as desired with one large and two small bells as a cluster. Position gold trim sections from the swag intersections down to and tucked underneath each bell. Pin gold trim in place. Remove the bells and machine zig-zag gold trim in place.

**8.** Position bells so the top of each bell is covering the gold trim and tuck the inner bell under the outer bell at the bottom. I arranged each bell at a slightly different angle for a natural appearance. Fuse in place following manufacturer's instructions.

**9.** Position bows, streamers and knot over the top of the swag intersections making sure to cover the top of the gold trim sections. Fuse in place following manufacturer's instructions.

**10.** Machine blanket-stitch around each bell and bow grouping to secure raw edges using matching thread.

**11.** Press on both sides to complete one appliqued border.

**12.** Repeat steps 6-11 to make a total of four appliqued borders.

**13.** On an ironing surface, press an H square flat. Measure 4″ down from one corner and draw orientation marks on adjacent sides. Position a corner swag in place aligning the outer top edges with the orientation marks. Fuse in place following manufacturer's instructions. Machine blanket stitch with matching thread.

**14.** Press on both sides to complete one border corner.

**15.** Repeat Steps 13-14 to make a total of four border corners.

## Quilt Top Assembly

**1.** Referring to project photo for orientation, stitch two appliqued borders to opposite sides of the quilt center; press.

**2.** Matching swag edges, sew two border corners on opposite ends of an applique border to make a top / bottom border unit; press. Repeat to make a second top / bottom border unit.

**3.** Aligning swag edges, sew top / bottom border units in place to complete the quilt top; press.

## Finishing the Quilt

**1.** Layer the quilt top, batting and backing and quilt as desired. The sample quilt was quilted with an allover pattern in the center section and custom quilted with straight lines around the appliques in the borders.

**2.** Stitch binding strips together end to end using diagonal seams. Fold and press the resulting long strip in half lengthwise with wrong sides together. Stitch to quilt, matching raw edges and mitering corners.

**3.** Fold the binding to the reverse side and hand- or machine-stitch in place.

**4.** Hand-stitch buttons or bells in place to represent a clapper on each appliqued bell.

# JINGLE BELLS WALL HANGING

Using the same swags and bells as the Jingle Bell Quilt, this smaller version is perfect for over the mantle or above a dresser or buffet.

## Jingle Bells Wall Hanging

CONFIDENT BEGINNER

**FINISHED RUNNER SIZE:** 10″ × 30″

### SUPPLIES

- Scraps – medium gold for bells; dark gold for inner bell
- 1 Fat quarter of red dot for bows & streamers
- 1 Fat quarter of green print for swag
- ½ yard off-white solid
- 1 yard of 40″ wide fabric for backing
- Batting to Size*
- Fusible web with Paper release*
- Template Material
- Thread to match appliques
- 9 – 4″ sections of ¼″ gold trim for hanging bells
- 9 – ½″ gold buttons or bells for clappers**
- Basic quilting tools and sewing supplies

\* Warm 80/20 Batting and Lite Steam-A-Seam 2 Fusible Web from The Warm Company was used to make the sample quilt.

\*\* Note: Buttons and bells can be choking hazards for both small children and pets. If the quilt will be used around either, they should be omitted.

### CUTTING INSTRUCTIONS

**From red dot:**
- Cut 5 (2½″ × 20″) binding strips.

**From off-white solid:**
- Cut 1 (10½″ × WOF) strip. Subcut strip into 1 (10½″ × 30½″) background rectangle.

BEDROOM
Jingle Bells Wall Hanging

## Assembling the Appliqued Row

**1.** Prepare templates for each applique motif provided. **Note:** the included applique templates are sized to scale.

**2.** Trace each shape onto the paper side of the fusible web referring to the number needed as listed in Step 4.

**3.** Cut out each shape leaving a ¼″ margin around each.

**4.** Fuse each shape onto the wrong side of the fabric as listed.

**GREEN PRINT:** 2 full swags and 2 half swags

**RED PRINT:** 6 bows, 3 reversed; 6 streamers, 3 reversed; 3 knots

**MEDIUM GOLD:** 3 large bells, 6 small bells

**DARK GOLD:** 3 large inner bells, 6 small inner bells

**5.** Cut out each shape on the drawn line and remove paper backing.

**6.** On an ironing surface, press the background rectangle flat. Measure 2½″ down from the top long side of the background rectangle and draw an orientation line. Referring to the photo for positioning, arrange full and half swags onto the background with the tips positioned along the orientation line. Fuse in place following manufacturer's instructions. Machine blanket stitch with matching thread.

**7.** Arrange bells as desired with one large and two small bells as a cluster. Position gold trim sections from the swag intersections down to and tucked underneath each bell. Pin gold trim in place. Remove the bells and machine zig-zag gold trim in place.

**8.** Position bells so the top of each bell is covering the gold trim and tuck the inner bell under the outer bell at the bottom. I arranged each bell at a slightly different angle for a natural appearance. Fuse in place following manufacturer's instructions.

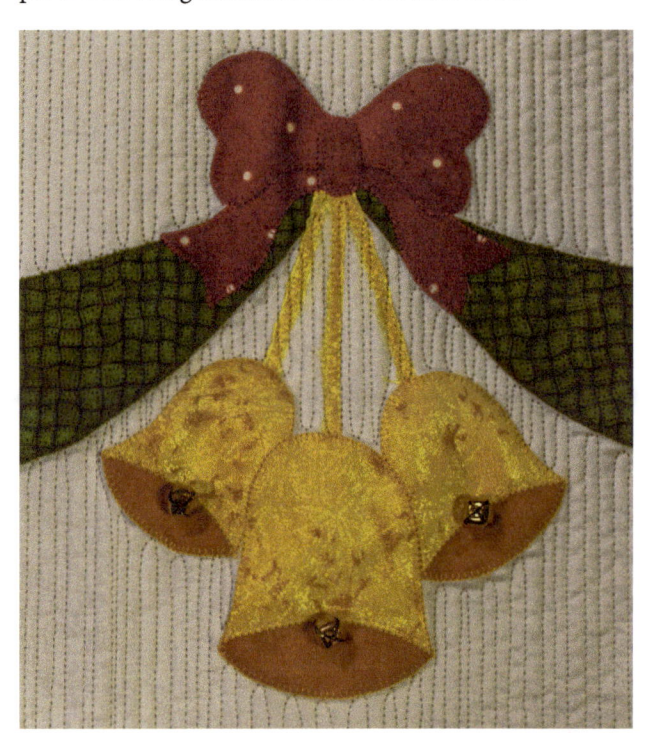

**9.** Position bows, streamers and knot over the top of the swag intersections making sure to cover the top of the gold trim sections. Fuse in place following manufacturer's instructions.

**10.** Machine blanket-stitch around each bell and bow grouping to secure raw edges using matching thread.

**11.** Press on both sides to complete one appliqued border.

## Finishing the Quilt

**1.** Layer the quilt top, batting and backing and quilt as desired. Sample quilt was quilted with straight lines around the appliques.

**2.** Stitch binding strips together end to end using diagonal seams. Fold and press the resulting long strip in half lengthwise with wrong sides together. Stitch to trimmed quilt, matching raw edges and mitering corners.

**3.** Fold the binding to the reverse side and hand- or machine-stitch in place.

**4.** Hand-stitch buttons or bells in place to represent a clapper on each appliqued bell.

BEDROOM
Jingle Bells Wall Hanging

LIVING ROOM

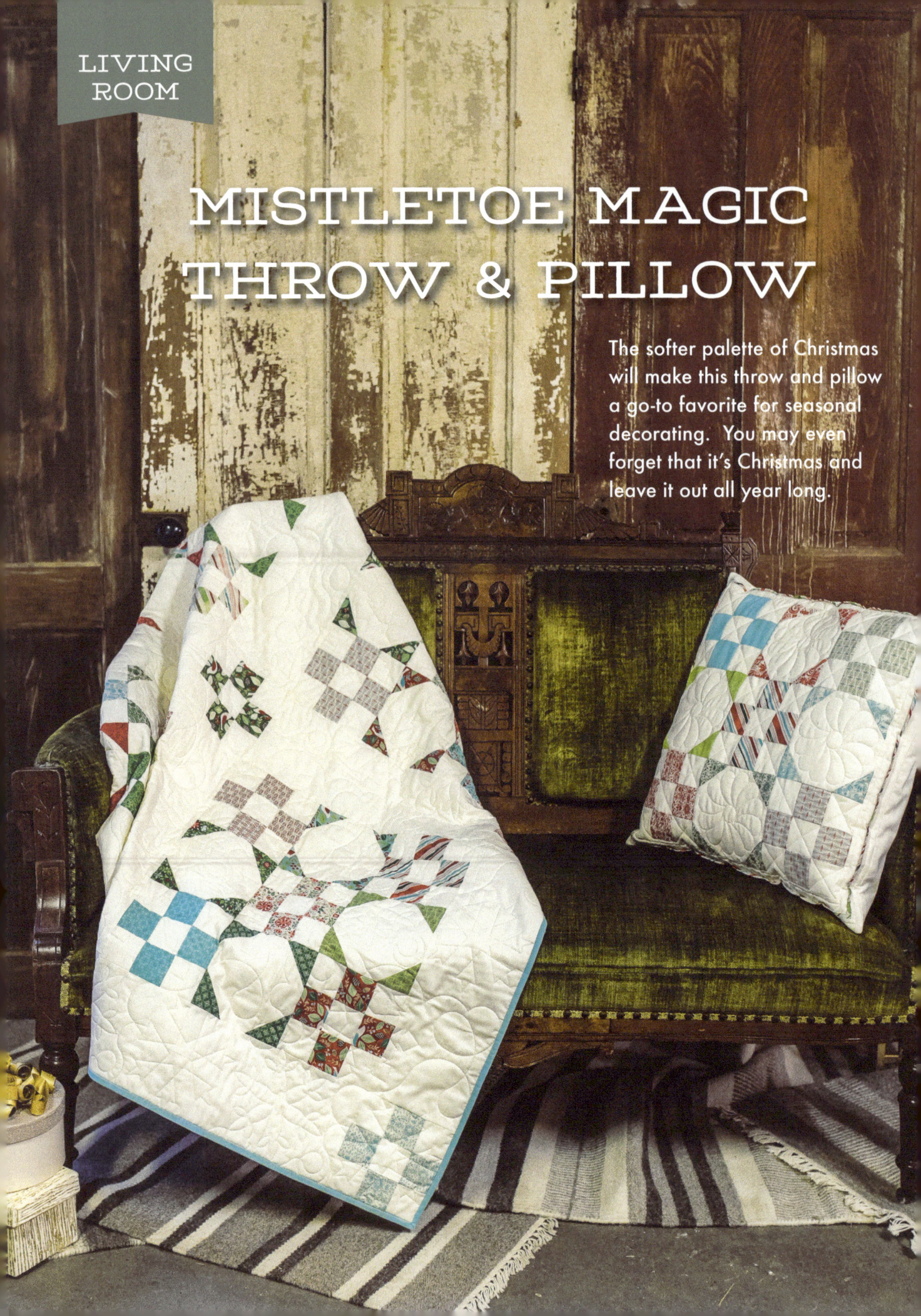

# MISTLETOE MAGIC THROW & PILLOW

The softer palette of Christmas will make this throw and pillow a go-to favorite for seasonal decorating. You may even forget that it's Christmas and leave it out all year long.

# Mistletoe Magic Throw & Pillow

BEGINNER

## QUILT

FINISHED SIZE: 54" × 54"   FINISHED BLOCK SIZE: 6" × 6"   NUMBER OF BLOCKS: 29 Nine-Patch, 16 Snowball

## PILLOW

FINISHED SIZE: 20" × 20"   FINISHED BLOCK SIZE: 6" × 6"   NUMBER OF BLOCKS: 5 Nine-Patch, 4 Snowball

## SUPPLIES

*To make both quilt and pillow*

- 1 package of 10" precut squares*
- ⅛ yard stripe*
- ½ yard of aqua tonal*
- 3⅓ yards of ivory solid
- 2½ yards of 40" wide fabric for backing
- Batting*
- Basic quilting tools and sewing supplies

*\* Evergreen Layer Cake and stripe, Grunge fabrics from Moda and Warm 80/20 batting from The Warm Company used to make sample quilt.*

## CUTTING INSTRUCTIONS

### QUILT

**From each of 29 different precut squares:**
- Cut 4 (2½") A squares

**From each of 16 different precut squares:**
- Cut 4 (2⅞") D squares

**From aqua tonal:**
- Cut 6 (2½" by WOF) binding strips

**From ivory solid:**
- Cut 2 (18½" by WOF) strips; subcut 12 (6½" × 18½") E rectangles
- Cut 10 (2½" × WOF) strips; subcut 145 (2½") B squares
- Cut 3 (6½" × WOF) strips; subcut 16 (6½") C squares

### 1 PILLOW

**From each of 5 different precut squares:**
- Cut 4 (2½") A squares

**From each of 4 different precut squares:**
- Cut 4 (2⅞") D squares

**From stripe:**
- Cut 2 (1" by WOF) J strips

**From ivory solid:**
- Cut 2 (2½" × WOF) strips; subcut strips into 25 (2½") B squares
- Cut 1 (6½" × WOF) strips; subcut strips into 4 (6½") C squares
- Cut 5 (1½" by WOF) strips; subcut strips into 2 (1½" × 18½") F, 2 (1½" × 20") G, 2 (1½" × 20") H and 2 (1½" × 22") I strips.
- Cut 1 (22" by WOF) strip; subcut strip into 2 (22" × 16") backing squares.

LIVING ROOM
Mistletoe Magic Throw & Pillow

## Block Construction

**1.** To make 1 Nine-Patch block, select four matching A squares and five B squares.

**2.** Arrange A and B squares into three rows of three squares each as shown.

**3.** Sew squares into rows and rows together to complete 1 nine-patch block; press.

**4.** Repeat steps 1-3 to make a total of 29 Nine-Patch blocks.

**5.** Draw a diagonal line from corner to corner on the wrong side of each D square.

**6.** To make 1 Snowball block, select four matching D squares and one C square.

**7.** With right sides together place a D square on one corner of a C square. Stitch on the drawn line; trim ¼″ away and press open.

**8.** Repeat stitching, trimming and pressing with a D square on each corner of the C square.

**9.** Repeat steps 6-8 to make a total of 16 Snowball blocks.

**10.** Select five Nine-Patch blocks and four Snowball blocks and arrange into three rows of three blocks each.

**11.** Sew blocks into rows and rows together to complete one nine-block square; press.

**12.** Repeat steps 10 – 11 to make a total of four nine-block squares.

## Quilt Top Assembly

**1.** Alternately arrange and sew four E rectangles and three nine-block squares to make a block row; press. Repeat to make three block rows.

**2.** Alternately arrange and sew four nine-patch blocks and three E rectangles to make a sashing row; press. Repeat to make four sashing rows.

**3.** Alternately sew sashing and blocks rows together to complete the quilt top; press.

LIVING ROOM
Mistletoe Magic Throw & Pillow   43

## Pillow Top Assembly

**1.** Referring to Steps 1 – 11 in Block Construction, make 5 Nine-Patch and 4 Snowball blocks and sew blocks together to complete the pillow top center; press.

**2.** Sew F strips to opposite sides and G strips to the top and bottom of the center; press.

**3.** Seam J strips on the short ends to make one long strip. Cut 4 (1″ × 20½″) flange strips.

**4.** Press each strip lengthwise with wrong sides together to make a flange strip.

**5.** With raw edges matching, baste flange strip on each side of pillow top.

**6.** Sew H strips over the flange to opposite sides and I strips to the top and bottom to complete the pillow top; press I strips away from the center and the flange towards the center.

## Finishing the Quilt

**1.** Layer the quilt top, batting and backing and quilt as desired. Sample quilt was quilted with an edge to edge pattern.

**2.** Stitch binding strips together end to end using diagonal seams. Fold and press the resulting long strip in half lengthwise with wrong sides together. Stitch to trimmed quilt, matching raw edges and mitering corners.

**3.** Fold the binding to the reverse side and hand- or machine-stitch in place.

## Finishing the Pillow

You can either quilt the pillow top before adding the back or leave it un-quilted. If you prefer to leave it un-quilted, skip Step 1.

**1.** If desired; layer block, right side up over batting and lining. Baste or pin. Quilt as desired. Sample was custom quilted with feather circles and cross-hatch. Trim batting and lining ¼″ beyond raw edge of block.

**2.** To make an envelope back for the pillow, press and stitch a ½″ double hem on one side of each backing square.

**3.** Place pillow front right side up and position one square at the top, right side down, matching top raw edges with a hemmed side toward the center. Place the second square at the bottom edge, right side down, matching raw edges at the bottom and overlapping the first square.

**4.** Stitch all around with a ⅜″ seam allowance. Turn right side out through the overlapped opening.

**5.** Insert the pillow form into the pillowcase to finish.

LIVING ROOM
Mistletoe Magic Throw & Pillow

45

# TREE OF PRESENTS WALL HANGING

Don't just put presents under the tree, but deck your walls with them too! Easy row piecing and a touch of appliqué makes this the perfect last minute project. This fun wall hanging is a super stash buster and adds a whimsical touch to your Holiday décor.

## Tree of Presents Wall Hanging

BEGINNER

FINISHED QUILT SIZE: 39″ × 41″

### SUPPLIES

Small pieces of the following fabrics:

- Brown (tree trunk), Red (star), Dark Green, Raspberry, Bright Blue, Dark Blue, Orange Metallic Dot, Light Aqua-Green, Red Metallic, Light Orange Dot, Orange Tonal, Light Blue, Medium Blue, Medium Green and Red / Gold Plaid
- ½ yard navy tonal
- 1⅓ yards blue tonal
- 1¼ yards of 40″ wide fabric for backing
- Batting to Size
- Basic quilting tools and sewing supplies

### CUTTING INSTRUCTIONS

From brown:
- Cut 1 (3½″ × 4″) Y rectangle

From dark green:
- Cut 1 (3″ × 20½″) X rectangle

From raspberry:
- Cut 1 each 2¼″ × 4″ M and 3¼″ × 7″ L rectangles

From bright blue:
- Cut 1 each 2¼″ × 3½″ N rectangle and 2¾″ × 8″ U rectangle

From dark blue:
- Cut 1 each 2¾″ × 7″ O and 2¼″ × 7″ Q rectangles

From orange metallic dot:
- Cut 1 (1″ × 7″) P strip

From light aqua-green:
- Cut 1 (4″ × 5″) R rectangle

From red metallic:
- Cut 1 each 3¾″ × 6″ S and 3″ × 3¾″ T rectangles

From light orange dot:
- Cut 1 (3″) K square,

From orange tonal:
- Cut 1 each 3¾″ × 5½″ V and 5½″ × 6″ W rectangles

From light blue:
- Cut 1 (4″ × 4¼″) DD rectangle

From medium blue:
- Cut 1 (4″ × 4¼″) Z rectangle

From medium green:
- Cut 4 (2½″ × 2¼″) BB squares

From red / gold plaid:
- Cut 1 (1½″ × 6″) CC and 2 (2″ × 2¼″) AA

From navy tonal:
- Cut 5 (2½″ by WOF) binding strips.

*Cutting Instructions, continued*

LIVING ROOM
Tree of Presents Wall Hanging        47

*Cutting Instructions, continued*

### From blue tonal:

- Cut 5 (5″ by WOF) strips; label one A and one J

  Subcut remaining strips into 2 each 5″ × 17½″ D, 5″ × 15½″ E, and 1 each 5″ × 15½″ I1 and 5″ × 13″ I2 strips.

- Cut 2 (4″ by WOF) strips; label one B.

  Subcut remaining strip into 2 (4″ × 19½″) H strips.

- Cut 2 (3″ by WOF) strips.

  Subcut strips into 2 each 3″ × 19½″ C and 3″ × 10½″ G strips.

  From remainder, subcut 2 (1½″ × 4¼″) EE strips.

## Assembling the Rows

### Row 3

**1.** Sew C strips to opposite sides of K square as shown to complete row 3: press.

### Row 4

**1.** Sew M and N together as shown to make an M-N unit; press. M-N unit should measure 2¼″ × 7″.

**2.** Sew L to the top of M-N to make a present unit; press. Present unit should measure 5″ × 7″.

**3.** Sew D strips to opposite sides of present unit to complete row 4: press.

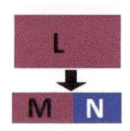

### Row 5

**1.** Sew O and Q strips to the opposite long sides of P to make a O-P-Q unit as shown; press seam allowances away from P. O-P-Q unit should measure 5″ × 7″.

**2.** Sew the R rectangle to the right hand side of O-P-Q unit to make a present unit; press. Present unit should measure 5″ × 10″.

**3.** Sew E strips to opposite sides of present unit to complete row 5: press.

## Row 6

**1.** Sew T and V rectangles together as shown to make a T-V unit; press. T-V unit should measure 3¾" × 8".

**2.** Sew U rectangle to the bottom of the T-V unit to make a T-U-V unit; press. T-U-V unit should measure 6" × 8".

**3.** Sew S and W rectangles to opposite sides of T-U-V unit to make a present unit; press. Present unit should measure 6" × 16¼".

**4.** Sew F strips to opposite sides of present unit to complete row 6: press.

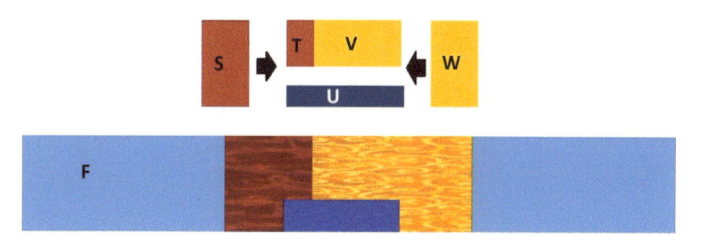

## Row 7

**1.** Sew G strips to opposite sides of X rectangle as shown to complete row 7: press.

## Row 8

**1.** Sew H strips to opposite sides of Y rectangle as shown to complete row 8: press.

## Row 9

**1.** Sew BB to opposite sides of an AA rectangle to make as shown to make an AA-BB row; press. Repeat to make a second AA-BB row. AA-BB row should measure 2¼" × 6".

**2.** Sew AA-BB rows to opposite sides of CC strip to make a center present; press seam allowances toward CC. Center present should measure 5" × 6".

**3.** Sew an EE strip to the top of Z to make a Z-EE unit; press. Z-EE unit should measure 5" × 4¼".

LIVING ROOM
Tree of Presents Wall Hanging

**4.** Sew an EE strip to the top of DD to make a EE-DD unit; press. EE-DD unit should measure 5″ × 4¼″.

**5.** Sew EE-DD and Z-EE units to opposite sides of center present to complete the present unit; press. Present unit should measure 5″ × 13½″.

**6.** Sew I1 and 12 strips to opposite sides of present unit to complete row 9: press.

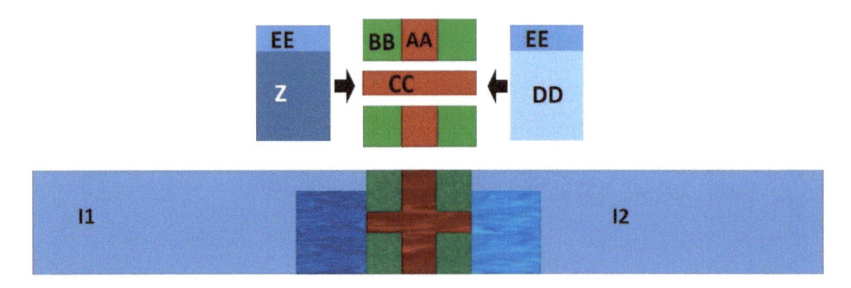

## Assembling the Quilt Top

**1.** Center and sew strips together in row order to complete the quilt top; press. **Note:** The edges may not lineup exactly and can be trimmed after quilting.
FIG A

## Adding Star Applique

**1.** Prepare applique motif piece from the provided insert using your preferred method. Note: the included applique template are sized to scale.

**2.** Trace the star motif onto the paper side of the fusible web.

**3.** Cut out leaving a ¼″ margin around all sides.

**4.** Following the manufacturer's directions, fuse applique piece to the wrong side of the red fabric. When complete you should have the following:

**1 STAR**

**5.** Cut the fabric-interfacing piece along the drawn line and remove paper backing.

**6.** On an ironing surface, press the pieced top, then arrange star applique at the top of the "tree" referring to the cover photo.

**7.** Fuse in place following manufacturer's instructions.

**8.** Stitch around star to secure raw edges. The cover quilt was stitched using matching thread and a machine applique (blanket) stitch.

**9.** Press both sides of the wall hanging top.

## Finishing the Quilt

**1.** Layer the quilt top, batting and backing and quilt as desired. Sample quilt was custom quilted with a straight line pattern.

**2.** Stitch binding strips together end to end using diagonal seams. Fold and press the resulting long strip in half lengthwise with wrong sides together. Stitch to trimmed quilt, matching raw edges and mitering corners.

**3.** Fold the binding to the reverse side and hand- or machine-stitch in place.

Row 1    **A**

Row 2    **B**

Row 3

Row 4

Row 5

Row 6

Row 7

Row 8

Row 9

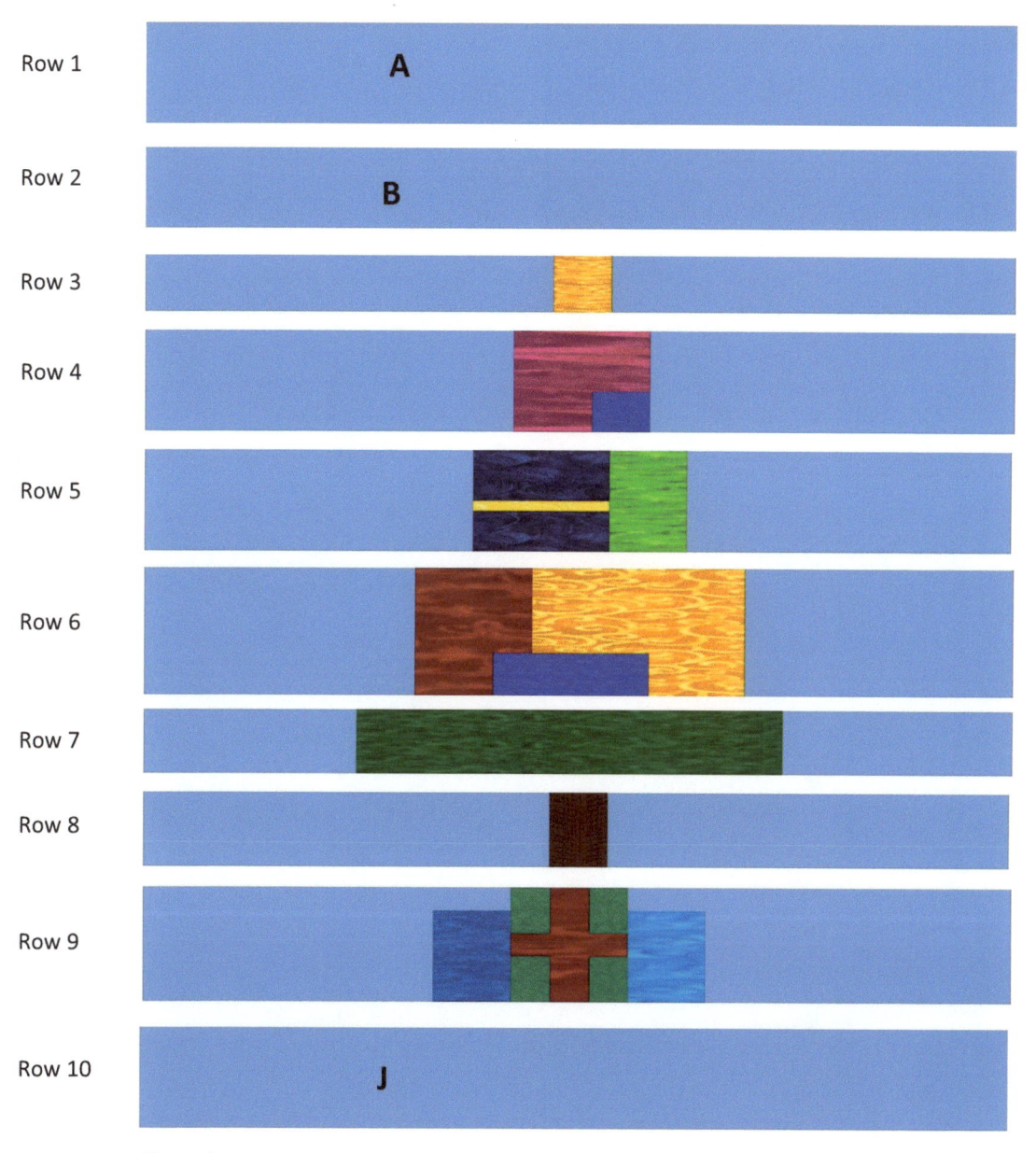

Row 10    **J**

Figure A

LIVING ROOM
Tree of Presents Wall Hanging

# O CHRISTMAS TREE WALL HANGING

The classic tree takes a modern flair with this sophisticated wall hanging. Change the look by using bright greens for a more whimsical appearance.

# O Christmas Tree Wall Hanging

CONFIDENT BEGINNER

FINISHED WALL HANING SIZE: 35″ × 40″   FINISHED BLOCK SIZE: 6″ × 6″   NUMBER OF BLOCKS: 15

## SUPPLIES

- Scrap of brown tonal
- ⅓ yard red tonal
- Scraps totaling ½ yard of assorted green tonals, prints and solids
- 1½ yards ivory solid
- 1¼ yards of 40″ wide fabric for backing
- Batting to size
- Thread
- Basic quilting tools and sewing supplies

## CUTTING INSTRUCTIONS

**From brown tonal**

- Cut 1 (2½″ × 4½″) L

**From red tonal**

- Cut 4 (2½″ by fabric width) binding strips

**From assorted greens**

- Cut 15 (2½″) D squares
- Cut 30 (2⅞″) B squares

**From ivory**

- Cut 3 (2⅞″ by fabric width) strips

  Subcut strips into 30 (2⅞″) A squares

- Cut 4 (2½″ by fabric width) strips

  Subcut strips into 60 (2½″) C squares

- Cut 4 (3″ by fabric width) strips

  Subcut strips into 2 (3″ × 35½″) K strips for top/bottom borders

  Subcut strips into 2 (3″ × 34½″) J strips for side borders

- Cut 1 (4½″ by fabric width) strips

  Subcut 2 (4½″ × 12½″) I strips

- Cut 2 (6½″ by fabric width) strips

  Subcut 2 each 6½″ × 12½″ E strips, 6½″ × 9½″ F strips, 6½″ × 6½″ G strips and 6½″ × 3½″ H strips.

LIVING ROOM
Christmas Tree Wall Hanging

## Block Construction

**1.** Draw a diagonal line from corner to corner on the wrong side of all A squares.

**2.** With right sides together, pair an A and B square together and stitch ¼″ from each side of drawn line. Cut on drawn line and press open to make two A-B units. Repeat to make a total of 60 A-B units.

**3.** Arrange and stitch A-B units on opposite sides of a C square to make an A-B-C row; press. Repeat to make a total of 30 A-B-C rows.

**4.** Arrange and stitch C squares on opposite sides of a D square to make a C-D row; press. Repeat to make 15 C-D rows.

**5.** Select two A-B-C rows and one C-D row. Referring to the block diagram, arrange and stitch rows together to complete one Churn Dash block; press. Repeat to make a total of 15 Churn Dash blocks.

## Assembling the Quilt Top

**1.** Sew E strips on opposite sides of a Churn Dash block to make Row A; press.

**2.** Sew two Churn Dash blocks and F strips together to make Row B; press.

**3.** Sew three Churn Dash blocks and G strips together to make Row C; press.

**4.** Sew four Churn Dash blocks and H strips together to make Row D; press.

**5.** Sew five Churn Dash blocks together to make Row E; press.

**6.** Sew I strips on opposite sides of a L strip to make Row F; press.

**7.** Sew Rows A-F together to complete the quilt center; press.

**8.** Sew J strips to opposite sides and K strips to the top and bottom to complete the quilt top; press. **FIG A**

## Finishing the Quilt

**1.** Layer the quilt top, batting and backing and quilt as desired. Cover quilt was custom quilted with block patterns and straight line quilting.

**2.** Stitch binding strips together end to end using diagonal seams. Fold and press the resulting long strip in half lengthwise with wrong sides together. Stitch to trimmed quilt, matching raw edges and mitering corners.

**3.** Fold the binding to the reverse side and hand- or machine-stitch in place.

Figure A

LIVING ROOM
Christmas Tree Wall Hanging  55

# CHRISTMAS FRIENDS THROW

Traditional Christmas reds and greens take center stage with throw that looks much more complex that it really is.

# Christmas Friends Throw

**CONFIDENT BEGINNER**

**FINISHED QUILT SIZE:** 60″ × 60″    **FINISHED BLOCK SIZE:** 8½″ × 8½″
**NUMBER OF BLOCKS:** 13 Star Blocks and 24 Setting squares

## SUPPLIES

- ¾ yards green solid*
- ¾ yards red solid*
- 2⅔ yards white solid*
- 3¾ yards of 40″ wide fabric for backing
- Batting to Size*
- Basic quilting tools and sewing supplies

*Kauffman Kona Solids in Snow, Cardinal and Pesto and Warm 80/20 batting by The Warm Company were used to make the sample quilt.*

## CUTTING INSTRUCTIONS

**From green:**
- Cut 1 (9¾″ by WOF) strip; Subut 3 (9¾″) squares; cut each square on both diagonals to make 12 I triangles
- Cut 2 (2½″ by WOF) strips; subcut strips into 25 (2½″) D squares

**From red solid:**
- Cut 7 (2½″ by WOF) binding strips
- Cut 3 (9¾″ by WOF) strips; subcut 9 (9¾″) squares; cut each square on both diagonals to make 36 G triangles
- Cut 3 (5⅛″ by WOF) strips; subcut 18 (5⅛″) squares; cut each square on one diagonal to make 36 E triangles.

**From white:**
- Cut 3 (9″ × WOF) strips; subcut 12 (9″) J squares
- Cut 3 (9¾″ by WOF) strips; subcut 12 (9¾″) squares; cut each square on both diagonals to make 48 H triangles
- Cut 2 (5⅛″ by WOF) strips; subcut 8 (5⅛″) squares; cut each square on one diagonal to make 16 F triangles.
- Cut 3 (2½″ by WOF) strips, subcut strips into 40 (2½″) A squares
- Cut 2 (2⅞″ by WOF) strips; subcut strips into 26 (2⅞″) B squares
- Cut 2 (2⅞″ by WOF) strips; subcut strips into 26 (2⅞″) C squares

LIVING ROOM
Christmas Friends Throw

# Block Construction

1. Draw a diagonal line from corner to corner on the wrong side of each B square.

2. With right sides together, pair an B and C square and stitch ¼″ on each side of the drawn line. Cut on the drawn line and press to make two B-C unit.

3. Repeat using all B and C squares to make a total of 52 B-C units.

4. To make one green friendship star block, select four A squares, four B-C units and one D squares and arrange into three rows of three squares each as shown.

5. Sew squares into rows and sew rows together to make one friendship star block; press.

6. Arrange and sew two E squares to opposite sides of the block; press. Sew two E squares to the remaining sides to complete a Block A; press.

7. Repeat steps 4-6 to make a total of 9 Block A's.

8. To make one white friendship star block, select four D squares, four B-C units and one A squares and arrange into three rows of three squares each as shown.

9. Sew squares into rows and sew rows together to make one friendship star block; press.

10. Arrange and sew two F squares to opposite sides of the block; press. Sew two F squares to the remaining sides to complete a Block B; press.

11. Repeat steps 8-10 to make a total of 4 Block B's.

12. Arrange and sew one each G and H triangles together to make a G-H unit; press. Repeat to make a total of 36 G-H units.

**13.** Select 24 G-H unit and arrange and sew two G-H units together to make a Block C; press. Repeat to make a total of 12 Block C's.

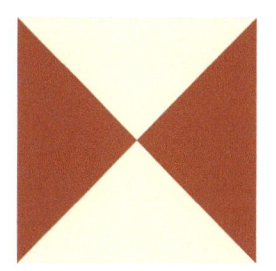

**14.** Repeat Step 12 using G and I triangles to make a total of 12 G-I units.

**15.** Arrange and sew a G-I and G-H unit to make a Block D. Repeat to make a total of 12 Block D's.

## Quilt Top Assembly

**1.** Referring to the Assembly Diagram for block placement, arrange the Blocks A, B, C and D blocks and J squares into 7 rows of 7 blocks each.

**2.** Sew blocks into rows and rows together to complete the quilt top; press.

## Finishing the Quilt

**1.** Layer the quilt top, batting and backing and quilt as desired. Sample quilt was custom quilted.

**2.** Stitch binding strips together end to end using diagonal seams. Fold and press the resulting long strip in half lengthwise with wrong sides together. Stitch to trimmed quilt, matching raw edges and mitering corners.

**3.** Fold the binding to the reverse side and hand- or machine-stitch in place.

LIVING ROOM
Christmas Friends Throw

# Templates

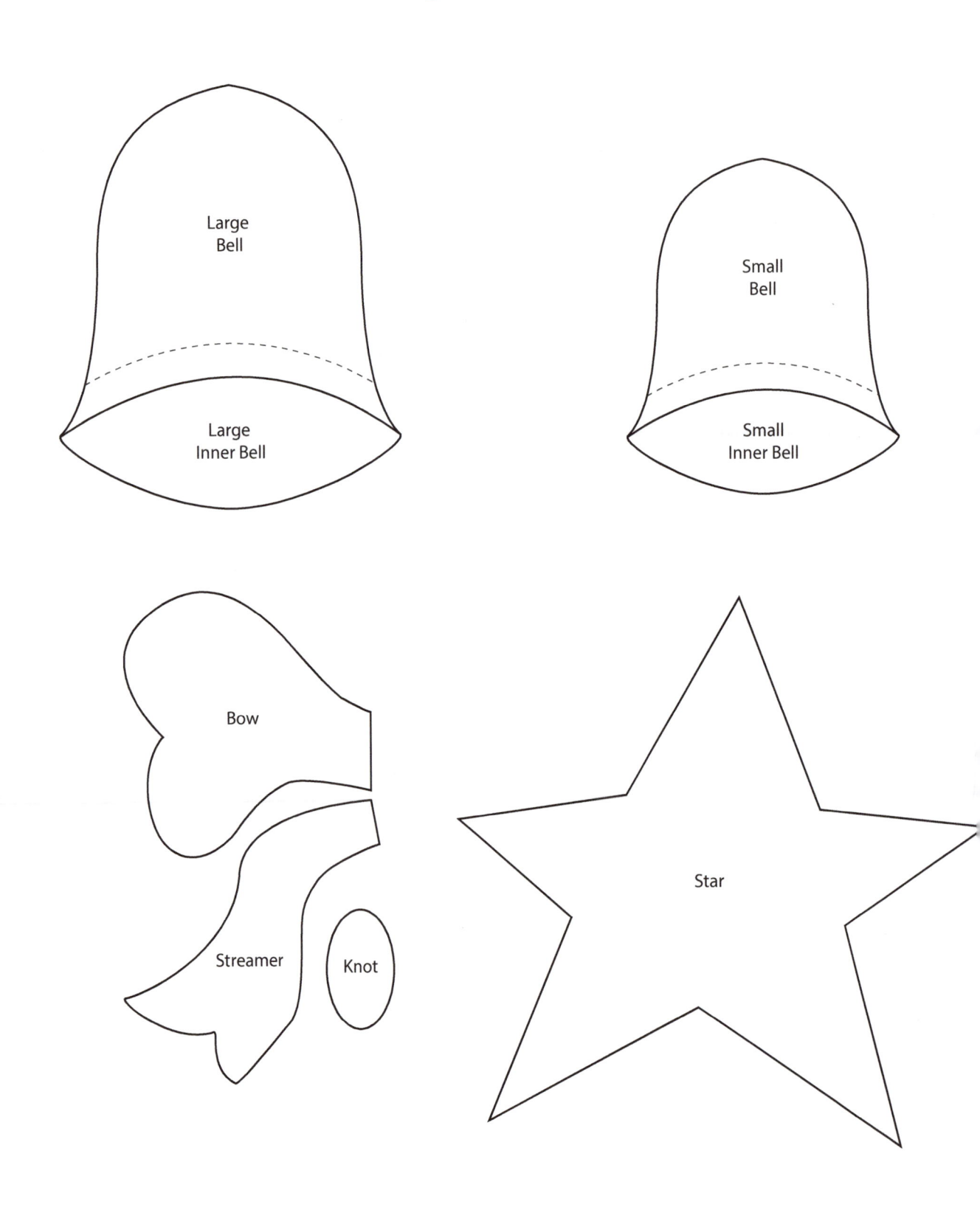

Large Bell

Large Inner Bell

Small Bell

Small Inner Bell

Bow

Streamer

Knot

Star

**60**  Masterpiece Quilting's 2018 Christmas Collection

Corner Swag

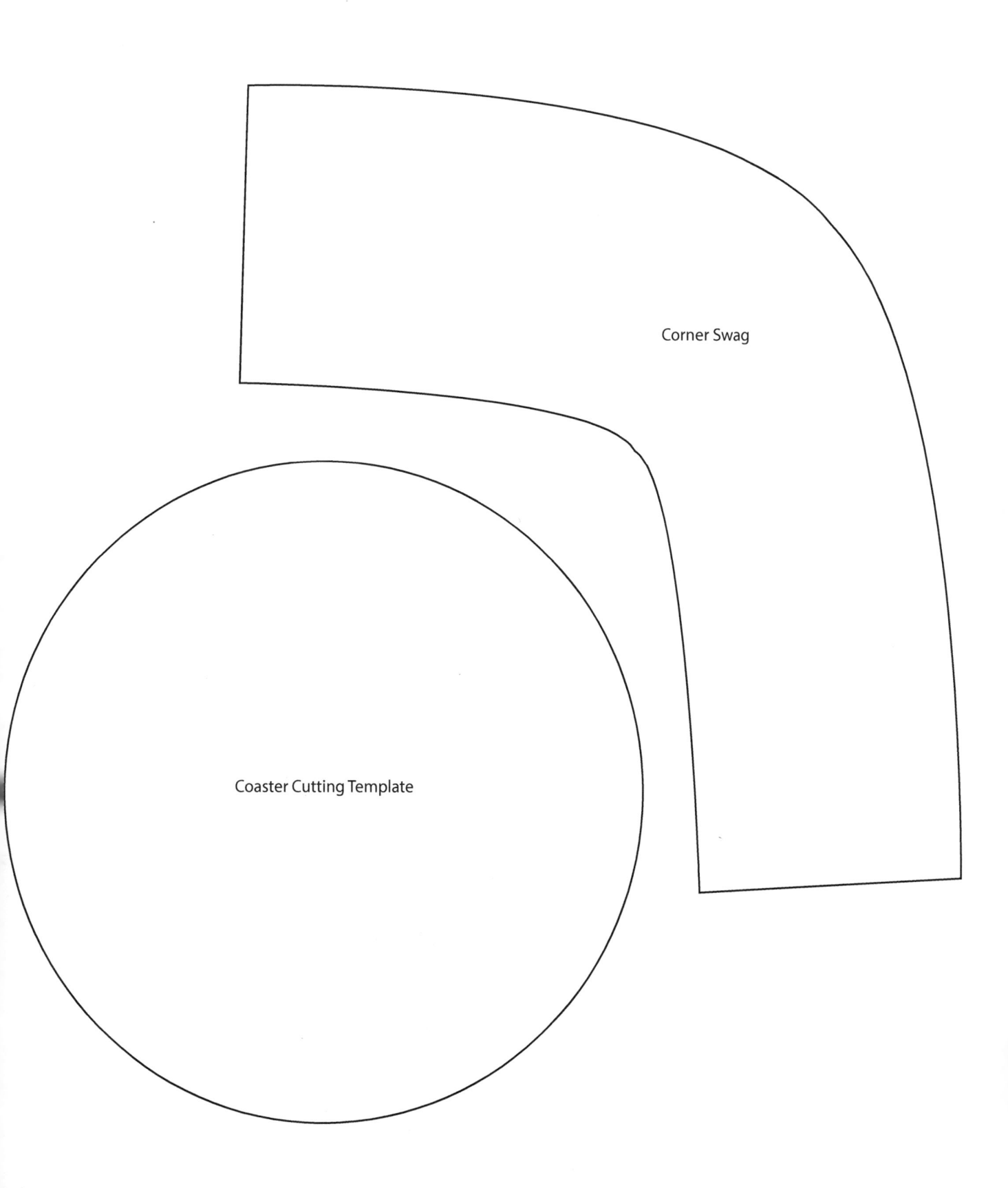

Coaster Cutting Template

Templates  **61**

Poinsettia Petal

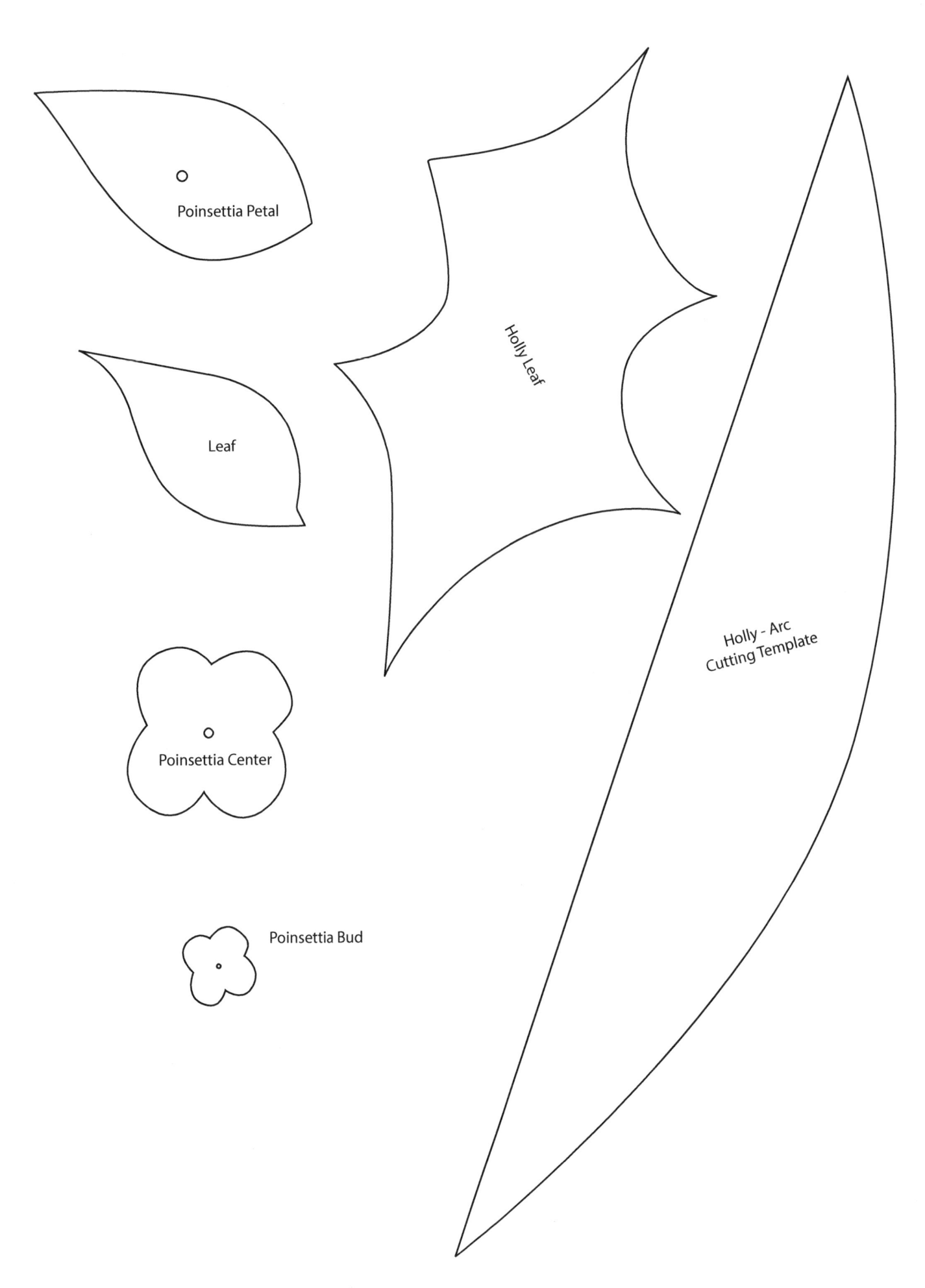

Leaf

Holly Leaf

Holly - Arc Cutting Template

Poinsettia Center

Poinsettia Bud

**62** Masterpiece Quilting's 2018 Christmas Collection

Runner Bow

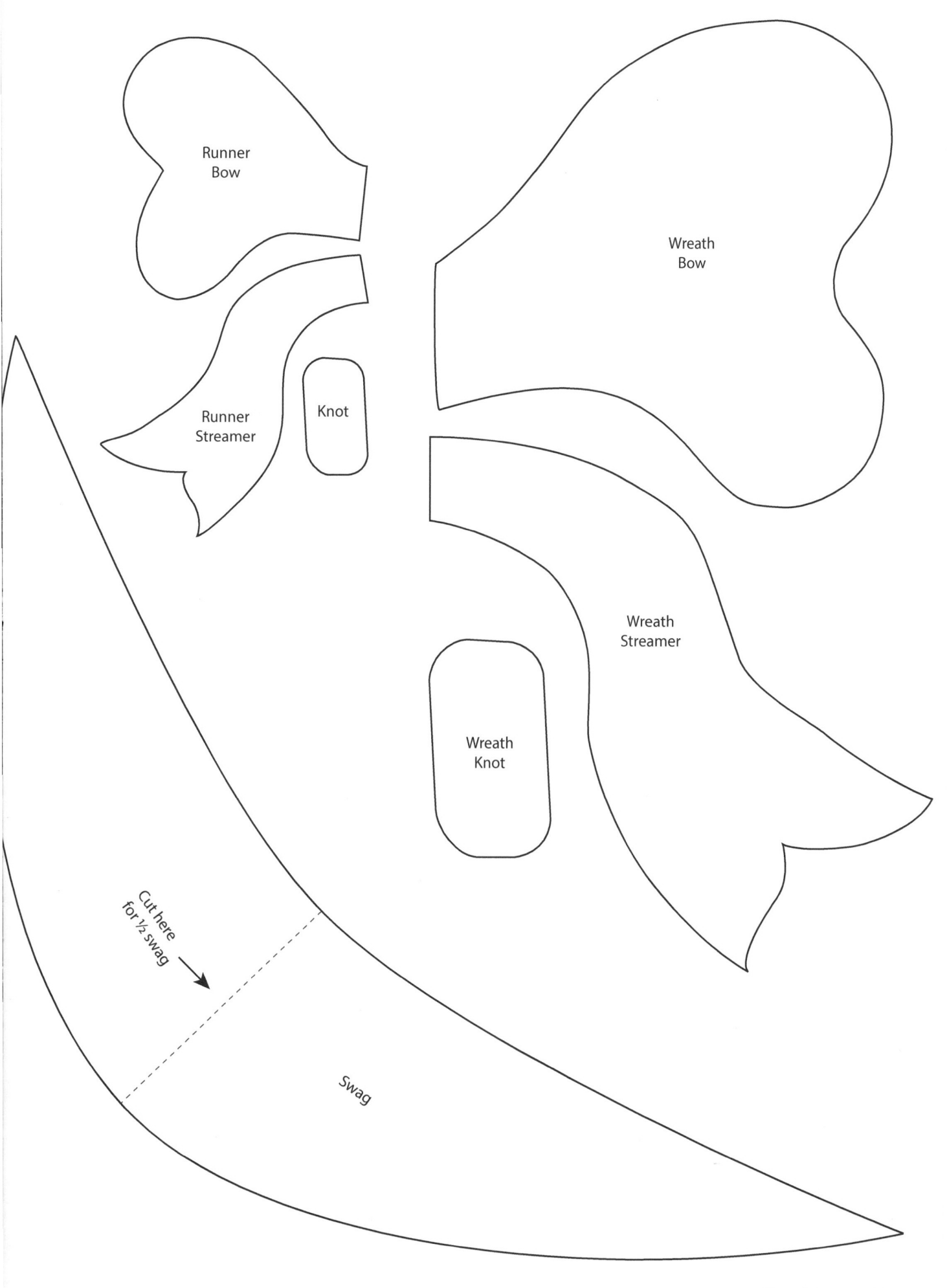

Wreath Bow

Runner Streamer

Knot

Wreath Streamer

Wreath Knot

Cut here for ½ swag

Swag

Templates **63**

## About the Author

Hi! I'm Nancy Scott and I own Masterpiece Quilting LLC.

I'm an author, designer and teacher who loves being crafty. Growing up in a family of "makers", I'm a proud DIY / MIY enthusiast. My current favorites include sewing & quilting, refinishing antiques, chalk-painting and photography. In 2006, I changed careers from the academia / corporate world and started my business Masterpiece Quilting LLC which has evolved to specialize in long-arm quilting, show quilts and custom-made memory quilts.

In 2012, I submitted my first design to a magazine for publication. It was accepted and my calling was found that day! Since then over 100 of my designs have been published in magazines, books, online and video classes and by fabric companies.

I use the inspiration of vintage quilts to design and create their modern soul mates. In addition to designing and quilting, I am also one of the quilting and sewing instructors for Annie's Creative Studio.